Handy Ohio Genealogy Handbook

By Gary L. Morris

©2015 Gary L. Morris

ISBN-13: 978-1507708408

ISBN-10: 1507708408

Table of Contents

Notes

Genealogical Research in Ohio

As it is one of the oldest American states, there are many genealogical records and resources available for tracing your family history in Ohio. Because there are so many records held at many different locations, tracking down the records for your ancestor can be an ominous task. Don't worry though, we know just where they are, and we'll show you which records you'll need, while helping you to understand:

1. What they are
2. Where to find them
3. How to use them

These records can be found both online and off, so we'll introduce you to online websites, indexes and databases, as well as brick-and-mortar repositories and other institutions that will help with your research in Ohio. So that you will have a more comprehensive understanding of these records, we have provided a brief history of the "Buckeye State" to illustrate what type of records may have been generated during specific time periods. That information will assist you in pinpointing times and locations on which to focus the search for your Ohio ancestors and their records.

A Brief History of Ohio

When the first Europeans entered Ohio in the 17th century the area was inhabited by the Native American tribes the Miami, the Shawnee, the Delaware, and the Wyandot. In total these tribes numbered about 15,000 people, and all of whom were hunters. The French were the first to explore the area, and they were joined by the English in the early 1700's. Most were traders who introduced tobacco, rum, alcohol, guns, and other weapons to the Indians in exchange for their furs and pelts.

Both the English and French initially claimed Ohio, the clash of ambitions leading to the French and Indian War which ended in the defeat of the French in 1763. The British controlled most of the region until the Revolutionary War after which possession was granted to the United States. In 1788 the first permanent settlement in Ohio was founded at Marietta by a group of Revolutionary war veterans who had received land warrants as a reward for their service. This settlement eventually became the city of Cincinnati.

Settlers flocked to the region via the Ohio River, which in turn created resistance from the Native American tribes. The native tribes raided villages, burned houses, and drove many settlers away. Military expeditions against the Native tribes were initially unsuccessful, until Major General "Mad Anthony" Wayne took control of forces in the area. Wayne built roads and established new forts in the area, eventually routing the allied tribesman with a crack squad of riflemen that he trained himself. The Native American tribes surrendered their claims to their land in the southern portion of Ohio at the Treaty of Greenville in 1795.

By 1802 the population of Ohio had grown enough so that it could seek statehood; finally granted on March 1, 1803. Native Americans still roamed free outside of Ohio's borders at this time however, and resistance against the white man's expansion was initiated by the Shawnee Chief Tecumseh. The Indians raided Toledo, though the action was repelled by militia led by Gen. William Henry Harrison, and Tecumseh was slain and resistance finally ended in October 1813.

The restoration of peace saw another population explosion in Ohio as settlers rushed to garb parcels of the rich, fertile soil, and to take advantage of the many economic opportunities the area offered. Immigrants from England, Ireland, and Germany arrived, snapping up the $1.25 per acre land. By 1850 Ohio was the third most populated state in the Union.

The Civil war divided Ohio as much as any other state. Pro-abolition New Englanders populated the northern counties, while the southern counties had ties to Kentucky and Virginia. This period saw rise to the "Copperheads," a group of anti-abolitionists who opposed President Lincoln's policies and urged loyalty to the Confederacy. The movement was strong enough to have Clement Vallandigham, head of the Copperheads, nominated as governor, though he was defeated by the Unionist John Brough. Ohio officially entered the war in 1863 when the Confederate general John Hunt Morgan led a cavalry force on raid through the southern counties.

The greatest generals to serve the Union cause, William Tecumseh Sherman, Ulysses S. Grant, and Philip H. Sheridan, came from Ohio, and each won crucial and decisive victories for the Union during the conflict.

Important Dates in Ohio History

1747 – Ohio Land Company of Virginia organized

1763 – Ceded by France to England

1778 – U.S. Army post built at Fort Laurens

1783 – England cedes Ohio Valley to the United States

1788 – First permanent settlement established at Marietta

1799 – Created as separate territory

1803 – Statehood

1863 – Enters Civil war

Famous Battles Fought in Ohio

There have been very few battles fought within the borders of modern day Ohio, and none during the Civil War. A few skirmishes took place during the War of 1812, the most notable being the **Siege of Fort Meigs.** There were also many battles fought in the area against Native American Indian tribes, the bloodiest being the **Battle on the Wabash,** fought in 1791.

These battle accounts that exist can be very effective in uncovering the military records of your ancestor. They can tell you what regiments fought in which battles, and often include the names and ranks of many officers and enlisted men.

Siege of Fort Meigs: http://www.fortmeigs.org/history/

Battle on the Wabash:
http://www.fortrecoverymuseum.com/history

Common Ohio Genealogical Issues and Resources to Overcome Them

Boundary Changes: Boundary changes are a common obstacle when researching Ohio ancestors. You could be searching for an ancestor's record in one county when in fact it is stored in a different one due to historical county boundary changes.

The **Atlas of Historical County Boundaries** can help you to overcome that problem. It provides a chronological listing of every boundary change that has occurred in the history of Ohio.

Atlas of Historical County Boundaries:
http://publications.newberry.org/ahcbp/documents/OH_Consolidated
_Chronology.htm#Consolidated_Chronology

Name Changes: Surname changes, variations, and misspellings can complicate genealogical research. It is important to check all spelling variations. Soundex, a program that indexes names by sound, is a useful first step, but you can't rely on it completely as some name variations result in different Soundex codes. The surnames could be different, but the first name may be different too. You can also find records filed under initials, middle names, and nicknames as well, so you will need to **get creative with surname variations** and spellings in order to cover all the possibilities. For help with surname variations read our instructional article on **How to Use Soundex**.

get creative with surname variations:
http://obituarieshelp.org/blog/?p=634

How to Use Soundex: http://obituarieshelp.org/blog/?p=505

Ohio Genealogical Organizations and Archives

Genealogical resources include not only records, but the organizations that house them, or can direct you to them. These institutions include: *Archives, Libraries, Genealogical Societies, Family History Centers, Universities, Churches, and Museums.*

Following are links to their websites, their physical addresses, and a summary of the records you can find there.

<u>Archives and Libraries</u>

Ohio Historical Society (State Archives) – muster rolls, county and state records, newspapers, maps, family papers, business and organizational records, historical photographs, death certificate index, birth records, census records, land records, marriage records, naturalization records

800 E. 17th Ave.
Columbus, OH 43211
Tel: (614) 297-2300

Ohio Historical Society: http://www.ohiohistory.org/collections--archives/archives-library/about-the-collection

National Archives Great Lakes Region – naturalization and immigration records, Native American records

7358 S. Pulaski Road
Chicago, IL 60629
Telephone: 773-948-9001
Fax: 773-948-9050

National Archives Great Lakes Region:
http://www.archives.gov/chicago/

Ohio Genealogical and Historical Societies

Genealogical and historical societies have access to extensive catalogues of genealogical data. They are also able to offer expert guidance for genealogical researchers. Many members are professional genealogists who are most willing to share their expertise in finding ancestors.

Ohio Genealogical Society – family histories, Civil War resources, cemetery index, birth, death, and marriages indexes (for members)

713 S. Main St.
P.O. Box 2625
Mansfield, OH 44907
Telephone: 419-756-7924
Fax: 419-756-8681

Ohio Genealogical Society: https://www.ogs.org/index.php

Western Reserve Historical Society - Census & Related Records, Religious Groups, Immigration & Ethnic Sources, Local Histories, Card Catalogs, Family Histories

10825 East Boulevard
Cleveland, OH 44106-1788
Telephone: 216-721-5722
Fax: 216-721-0645

Western Reserve Historical Society:
http://www.wrhs.org/Research/Family_History

Ohio Mailing Lists

Mailing lists are internet based facilities that use email to distribute a single message to all who subscribe to it. When information on a particular surname, new records, or any other important genealogy information related to the mailing list topic becomes available, the subscribers are alerted to it. Joining a mailing list is an excellent way to stay up to date on Ohio genealogy research topics. Rootsweb have an extensive listing of **Ohio Mailing Lists** on a variety of topics.

Ohio Mailing Lists:
http://lists.rootsweb.ancestry.com/index/usa/OH/misc.html

Ohio Message Boards

A message board is another internet based facility where people can post questions about a specific genealogy topic and have it answered by other genealogists. If you have questions about a surname, record type, or research topic, you can post your question and other researchers and genealogists will help you with the answer. Be sure to check back regularly, as the answers are not emailed to you. The Ohio message boards at **Rootsweb** are completely free to use.

Rootsweb:
http://boards.rootsweb.com/localities.northam.usa.states/mb.ashx

Ohio Newspapers and Periodicals

Many genealogy periodicals and historical newspapers contain reprinted copies of family genealogies, transcripts of family Bible records, information about local records and archives, census indexes, church records, queries, land records, obituaries, court records, cemetery records, and wills. The following sites have historical Ohio newspapers and periodicals that you can search online or on-site.

Ohio Historical Society (State Archives) – historical Ohio newspapers dating from 1793

800 E. 17th Ave.
Columbus, OH 43211
Tel: (614) 297-2300

Ohio Historical Society: http://www.ohiohistory.org/collections--archives/archives-library/about-the-collection

GenealogyBank.com – free searchable database of Ohio newspaper archives, 1801–1991

GenealogyBank.com:
http://www.genealogybank.com/gbnk/newspapers/explore/USA/Ohio/

Library of Congress Digital Newspaper Directory – free searchable database of historical U.S. newspapers dating from 1690-present

Library of Congress Digital Newspaper Directory:
http://chroniclingamerica.loc.gov/search/titles/

NewspaperArchive.com – largest online database of historical newspapers in the world.

NewspaperArchive.com: http://newspaperarchive.com/

Historical Ohio Maps and Gazetteers

Maps are an integral part of genealogical research. They help us to locate landmarks, towns, cities, parishes, states, provinces, waterways and roads and streets. They also help us to determine when and where boundary changes might have taken place, and give us a visualization of the area we're researching in.

For locating place names, a gazetteer is the best possible resource for any genealogist. Gazetteers are also sometimes called "place name dictionaries", and can help you to locate the area in which you need to conduct research. Below are links to the maps and gazetteers for research in Ohio.

Peabody GNIS Service – Ohio:
http://peabody.research.yale.edu/cgi-bin/Query.GNIS?ST=Ohio&SU=1

Color Landform Atlas – Ohio:
http://fermi.jhuapl.edu/states/oh_0.html

1985 U.S. Atlas: http://www.livgenmi.com/1895/OH/

Ohio Hometown Locator: http://ohio.hometownlocator.com/

Ohio City Directories

City directories are similar to telephone directories in that they list the residents of a particular area. The difference though is what is important to genealogists, and that is they pre-date telephone directories. You can find an ancestor's information such as their street address, place of employment, occupation, or the name of their spouse. A one-stop-shop for finding city directories in Ohio is the **Ohio Online Historical Directories** which contains a listing of every available online historical directory related to Ohio.

Ohio Online Historical Directories:
https://sites.google.com/site/onlinedirectorysite/Home/usa/oh

Additionally the **Public Libraries of Cincinnati Virtual Library** has an online database of almost one thousand directories from the years 1819 through 1941

Public Libraries of Cincinnati Virtual Library:
http://virtuallibrary.cincinnatilibrary.org/virtuallibrary/vl_citydir.asp x

Ohio Genealogical Records

<u>Birth, Death, Marriage and Divorce Records</u> – Also known as vital records, birth, death, and marriage certificates are the most basic, yet most important records attached to your ancestor. The reason for their importance is that they not only place your ancestor in a specific place at a definite time, but potentially connect the individual to other relatives. Below is a list of repositories and websites where you can find Ohio vital records.

Ohio Department of Health - birth certificates, death certificates, fetal death certificates, marriage and divorce abstracts, and confidential abortion reports.

Ohio Department of Health
Center for Vital and Health Statistics
246 North High Street
Columbus, OH 43215
Tel: 614-466-2531
Email: vitalstat@odh.ohio.gov

Ohio Department of Health :
http://www.odh.ohio.gov/healthstats/vitalstats/vitalstatsmainpage.aspx

Ohio Historical Society (State Archives) – birth records from several Ohio counties between 1867 and 1908, Online Death Certificate index, 1913-1944, county marriage records dating from 1895.

800 E. 17th Ave.
Columbus, OH 43211
Tel: (614) 297-2300

Ohio Historical Society: http://www.ohiohistory.org/collections--archives/archives-library/about-the-collection

Ohio Genealogical Society – Ohio Birth Index, 1940-1998, Ohio Divorce Index, 1962-1996, Ohio Marriage Index, 1789-1830, Ohio Marriage Index, 1970-1990

713 S. Main St.
P.O. Box 2625
Mansfield, OH 44907
Telephone: 419-756-7924
Fax: 419-756-8681

Ohio Genealogical Society: https://www.ogs.org/index.php

Family Search has the following indexes which can be searched online for free:

Ohio, Births and Christenings, 1821-1962:
https://familysearch.org/search/collection/1680845

Ohio, County Births, 1841-2003:
https://familysearch.org/search/collection/1932106

Ohio, County Marriages, 1789-1994:
https://familysearch.org/search/collection/1614804

Ohio, Death Index, 1908-1932, 1938-1944, and 1958-2007:
https://familysearch.org/search/collection/1949341

Ohio, Deaths and Burials, 1854-1997:
https://familysearch.org/search/collection/1681000

Ohio, Deaths, 1908-1953:
https://familysearch.org/search/collection/1307272

Ohio, Marriages, 1800-1958:
https://familysearch.org/search/collection/1681001

Census Reports

Census records are among the most important genealogical documents for placing your ancestor in a particular place at a specific time. Like BDM records, they can also lead you to other ancestors, particularly those who were living under the authority of the head of household.

Federal census records for Ohio exist from 1820–1930 and can be found at:

Ohio Historical Society (State Archives) – Federal Census Returns for the State of Ohio 1820-1880 and 1900-1930; Indexes to Federal Census records from 1820-1880 and 1900-1920

800 E. 17th Ave.
Columbus, OH 43211
Tel: (614) 297-2300

Ohio Historical Society: http://www.ohiohistory.org/collections--archives/archives-library/about-the-collection

National Archives – Federal census Schedules for all states, 1790-1940

8601 Adelphi Road
College Park, MD 20740-6001
Tel: 1-866-272-6272

National Archives: http://www.archives.gov/research/census/

The **Free Census Project** has transcribed many Ohio indexes and new material is added daily

Free Census Project: http://usgwcensus.org/cenfiles/oh.htm

Access Genealogy – Ohio county census records dating from 1820

Access Genealogy: http://www.accessgenealogy.com/census/ohio-census-records.htm

African American Census Schedules Online – slave schedules, mortality schedules, slave-owners census

African American Census Schedules Online:
http://www.afrigeneas.com/aacensus/ga/

Native Americans in Census Records (US National Archives)

Native Americans in Census Records:
http://www.archives.gov/research/census/native-americans/

Ohio Church Records

Church and synagogue records are a valuable resource, especially for baptisms, marriages, and burials that took place before 1900. You will need to at least have an idea of your ancestor's religious denomination, and in most cases you will have to visit a brick and mortar establishment to view them.

Most church records are kept by the individual church, although in some denominations, records are placed in a regional archive or maintained at the diocesan level. Local Historical Societies are sometimes the repository for the state's older church records. Below are links archives that maintain church records, as well as a few databases that can be viewed online.

The **Family History Library** contains many church records from a variety of denominations on microfilm.

Family History Library:
http://familysearch.org/learn/wiki/en/Family_History_Library

Central Repositories for Denominational Records

Church of Jesus Christ of Latter-day Saints (Mormons)

Early Mormon Church records for Ohio can be found on film located at the LDS Family History Library in Salt Lake City and can be searched via the **Family History Library Catalog**

Family History Library Catalog:
https://familysearch.org/eng/Library/FHLC/frameset_fhlc.asp

Baptist

Baptist Historical Collection
Z. Smith Reynolds Library
Wake Forest University
P.O. Box 7777
Winston-Salem, NC 27109-7777
Telephone: 336-758-5089
Fax: 336-758-5605

Baptist Historical Collection:
http://wakespace.lib.wfu.edu/handle/10339/33589

Presbyterian

Presbyterian Historical Society
United Presbyterian Church in the USA
425 Lombard Street
Philadelphia, Pennsylvania 19147
Telephone: (215) 627-1852

Presbyterian Historical Society: http://www.history.pcusa.org/

Methodist

United Methodist Church Archives
P.O. Box 127 Drew University
36 Madison Ave.
Madison, NJ 07940-3189
Telephone: 973-408-3189
Fax: 973-408-3909
E-mail: research@gcah.org

United Methodist Church Archives:
http://www.gcah.org/site/c.ghKJI0PHIoE/b.2858857/k.BF4D/Home.
htm

<u>Roman Catholic</u>

Archdiocese of Cincinnati
Chancery
100 E. Eighth Street
Cincinnati, OH 45202
Telephone: 513-421-3131
Fax: 513-421-6225

Archdiocese of Cincinnati: http://www.catholiccincinnati.org/

Diocese of Columbus

Chancery Office
198 East Broad Street
Columbus, OH 43215
Telephone: 614-224-2251
Fax: 614-224-6306 3

Diocese of Columbus: http://www.colsdioc.org/

Diocese of Cleveland

Chancery Building
1027 Superior Ave.
Cleveland, OH 44114
Telephone: 216-696-6525
Fax: 216-621-7332

Diocese of Cleveland: http://www.dioceseofcleveland.org/

Diocese of Steubenville

422 Washington Street
P.O. Box 969
Steubenville, OH 43952
Telephone: 740-282-0728

Diocese of Steubenville: http://www.diosteub.org/

Diocese of Toledo

1933 Spielbusch Ave
Toledo, OH 43604
Telephone: 419-244-6711
Fax: 419-244-4791

Diocese of Toledo: http://www.toledodiocese.org/

Diocese of Youngstown
Chancery Office
144 West Wood Street
Youngstown, OH 44503
Telephone: 216-744-8451
Fax: 216-744-8451/744-2848

Diocese of Youngstown: http://www.doy.org/

Society of Friends

Ohio Yearly Meeting of the Society of Friends

Olney Friends School
61830 Sandy Ridge Road
Barnesville, OH 43713
Telephone: 740-425-3655
Fax: 740-425-3202

Evangelical Friends Church, Eastern Division

5350 Broadmoor Circle, N.W.
Canton, OH 44709
Telephone: 330-493-1660
Fax: 330-493-0852

Evangelical Friends Church, Eastern Division:
https://www.efcer.org/

Ohio Military Records

More than 40 million Americans have participated in some time of war service since America was colonized. The chance of finding your ancestor amongst those records is exceptionally high. Military records can even reveal individuals who never actually served, such as those who registered for the two World Wars but were never called to duty.

Below are a number of links to websites and archives that contain Ohio military records.

Ohio Historical Society (State Archives) – Civil War, Ohio National Guard, the Spanish American War, and World War I ledgers, muster rolls, telegrams, and correspondence, Special Veteran's Census,1890, Census of surviving Union veterans of the Civil War or their widows, Graves Registration File, Military Rosters - Revolutionary War through World War I

800 E. 17th Ave.
Columbus, OH 43211
Tel: (614) 297-2300

Ohio Historical Society: http://www.ohiohistory.org/collections--archives/archives-library/about-the-collection

University of Akron – Grand Army of the Republic records, rosters, correspondences, certificates

Akron, OH 44325
Phone: 330-972-7111

University of Akron:
http://www.uakron.edu/libraries/archives/collections/categories/?cat=e0c2ba28-93bd-433e-b179-39a73edc736e

US Department of Veterans Affairs Nationwide Gravesite Locator – includes information on veterans and their family members buried in veterans and military cemeteries having a government grave marker.

US Department of Veterans Affairs Nationwide Gravesite Locator: http://gravelocator.cem.va.gov/

You may also find your ancestor's military records in the following databases:

United States General Index to Pension Files, 1861-1934: https://familysearch.org/search/collection/1919699

United States Index to Service Records, War with Spain, 1898

United States Index to Service Records, War with Spain, 1898: https://familysearch.org/search/collection/1919583

United States Index to Indian Wars Pension Files, 1892-1926 – military pension records of soldiers who fought in the Indian Wars between 1817 and 1898

United States Index to Indian Wars Pension Files, 1892-1926: https://familysearch.org/search/collection/1979427

United States Registers of Enlistments in the U.S. Army, 1798-1914 - index of men who enlisted in the United States Army, 1798-1914.

United States Registers of Enlistments in the U.S. Army, 1798-1914: https://familysearch.org/search/collection/1880762

United States Mexican War Pension Index, 1887-1926 - index to Mexican War pension files for service between 1846 and 1848

United States Mexican War Pension Index, 1887-1926: https://familysearch.org/search/collection/1979390

Civil War Soldiers Service Records - Service records for both Union and Confederate soldiers indexed by soldier's name, rank, and unit.

Civil War Soldier Service Records:
http://go.fold3.com/civilwar_records/

Ohio Cemetery Records

As convenient as it is to search cemetery records online, keep in mind that there are a few disadvantages over visiting a cemetery in person. They are:

- Tombstone information is not always accurately transcribed
- The arrangement of the graves in a cemetery can be crucial as family members are often buried next to each other or in the same grave. This arrangement is not always preserved in the alphabetical indexes that are found online.

With that information in mind, the following websites have databases that can be searched online for Ohio Cemetery records.

Ohio Genealogical Society – Ohio Cemetery Locations Free Index

713 S. Main St.
P.O. Box 2625
Mansfield, OH 44907
Telephone: 419-756-7924
Fax: 419-756-8681

Ohio Genealogical Society:
https://www.ogs.org/research/search_cemepublic.php

Ohio Tombstone Transcription Project - death and burial records

Ohio Tombstone Transcription Project:
http://www.usgwtombstones.org/ohio/ohio.html

African American Cemeteries Online – African American, slave, and Native American cemetery records

African American Cemeteries Online:
http://africanamericancemeteries.com/ar/

Access Genealogy – database of Ohio cemetery record transcriptions

Access Genealogy:
http://www.accessgenealogy.com/cemetery/ohio-cemetery-records.htm

Find a Grave – over 100 million grave records can be searched on this site. Search can be conducted by name, location, or cemetery name.

Find a Grave: http://www.findagrave.com/

Interment.net - A free online database containing approximately 4 million cemetery records from around the world.

Interment.net: http://www.interment.net/

Billion Graves – as the name implies, you can search a billion records including headstone photos, transcriptions, cemetery records, and grave locations.

Billion Graves link to:
http://billiongraves.com/pages/search/index.php#cemetery

Ohio Obituaries

Obituaries can reveal a wealth about our ancestor and other relatives. You can search our **Ohio Obituaries Listings** from hundreds of Ohio newspapers online for free.

Ohio Obituaries Listings:
http://obituarieshelp.org/ohio_newspaper_obituaries.html

Ohio Wills and Probate Records

The documents found in a probate packet may include a complete inventory of a person's estate, newspaper entries, witness testimony, a copy of a will, list of debtors and creditors, names of executors or trustees, names of heirs. They can not only tell you about the ancestor you're currently researching, but lead to other ancestors.

Probate records in Ohio were kept in **Ohio County Courts** from the time of each county's creation.

Ohio County Courts: http://www.ohiocourtlinks.org/

Tou can also find Ohio probate records at:

Ohio Historical Society (State Archives) – Will Packets, 1800-1944; Probate Records, 1849-1854; OHIO Association of Probate Judges records, 1910-1956; Court Journals, Individual County Probate records and more

800 E. 17th Ave.
Columbus, OH 43211
Tel: (614) 297-2300

Ohio Historical Society: http://www.ohiohistory.org/collections--archives/archives-library/about-the-collection

Family Search has the following online indexes which can be searched for free:

Ohio, Cuyahoga County Probate Files, 1813-1917:
https://familysearch.org/search/collection/1837736

Ohio, Cuyahoga County Records, 1880-1950:
https://familysearch.org/search/collection/1908531

Ohio, Geauga County Records, 1887-1970:
https://familysearch.org/search/collection/2134457

Ohio, Jefferson County Court Records, 1797-1940:
https://familysearch.org/search/collection/1935519

Ohio, Montgomery County, Probate Estate Files, 1850-1900:
https://familysearch.org/search/collection/1916172

Ohio, Probate Records, 1789-1996:
https://familysearch.org/search/collection/1992421

Ohio, Stark County Court Records, 1809-1917:
https://familysearch.org/search/collection/1878534

Ohio, Stark County Probate Records, 1886-1921:
https://familysearch.org/search/collection/1928108

Ohio, Trumbull County Court Records, 1795-2010:
https://familysearch.org/search/collection/2065327

<u>Ohio Immigration and Naturalization Records</u>

The naturalization process generated many types of records, including petitions, declarations of intention, and oaths of allegiance. These records can provide family historians with information such as a person's birth date and place of birth, immigration year, marital status, spouse information, occupation, witnesses' names and addresses, and more.

Ohio Historical Society (State Archives) – county naturalization records for some Ohio counties between 1790 and 1917.

800 E. 17ᵗʰ Ave.
Columbus, OH 43211
Tel: (614) 297-2300

Ohio Historical Society: http://www.ohiohistory.org/collections--archives/archives-library/about-the-collection

National Archives Great Lakes Region – naturalization and immigration records, 1851- 1991

7358 S. Pulaski Road
Chicago, IL 60629
Telephone: 773-948-9001
Fax: 773-948-9050

National Archives Great Lakes Region:
http://www.archives.gov/chicago/

Family Search has the following online indexes which can be searched for free:

Ohio, County Naturalization Records, 1800-1977:
https://familysearch.org/search/collection/1987615

Ohio, Southern District Naturalization Index, 1852-1991:
https://familysearch.org/search/collection/2110749

Ohio Native American Records

National Archives Great Lakes Region – Mt. Pleasant Indian School and Agency Student Case Files, 1893-1946

7358 S. Pulaski Road
Chicago, IL 60629
Telephone: 773-948-9001
Fax: 773-948-9050
Wewbsite: http://www.archives.gov/chicago/

Access Genealogy – Ohio Native American census records, tribal histories, and much more:
http://www.accessgenealogy.com/native/ohio-indian-tribes.htm

U.S. National Archives - information on American Indians who maintained their ties to Federally-recognized Tribes (1830-1970).

U.S. National Archives: http://www.archives.gov/research/native-americans/

Records of the Bureau of Indian Affairs (BIA)

Records of the Bureau of Indian Affairs (BIA):
http://www.archives.gov/research/guide-fed-records/groups/075.html

American Indians Records Repository - records dating from the 1700s including trust, education and other historic Indian Affairs records

American Indian Records Repository
Meritex Enterprises
17501 West 98th Street
Lenexa, KS 66219
Phone: 913-888-0601

American Indians Records Repository:
http://www.doi.gov/ost/records_mgmt/american-indian-records-repository.cfm

Missing Matriarchs – Resources for Researching Female Ohio Ancestors

Looking for female ancestors requires an adjustment of how we view traditional records sources. A woman's identity was often under that of her husband, and often individual records for them can be difficult to locate. The following resources are effective in locating female ancestors in Ohio where traditional records may not reveal them.

Bibliographies

- *Women in Ohio History,* Marta Whitlock (Ohio Historical Society, 1976)
- *Remember the Ladies: A Bibliography on Women in Montgomery County History,* Dayton and Montgomery County Public Library, 1986)
- *Women in Cleveland: An Illustrated History,* Marian J. Morton (Indiana University Press, 1995)
- *Quilts in Community: Ohio's Traditions,* Ricky Clark (Rutledge Hill Press, 1991)

Selected Resources for Ohio Women's History

Center for Women's Studies
University of Cincinnati
155 McMicken Hall
Cincinnati, OH 45221-0164

Women's Studies Archives
Jerome Library
Bowling Green State University
Bowling Green, OH 34303

William O. Thompson memorial Library
Ohio State University
1800 Cannon Drive
Columbus, OH 43210

Common Ohio Carolina Surnames

The following surnames are among the most common in Ohio and are also being currently researched by other genealogists. If you find your surname here, there is a chance that some research has already been performed on your ancestor.

ABNER, ABSALOM, ADAMS, AGNER, AMMERMAN, ARMSTRONG, ASHINGER, AYRES, BAILEY, BAKER, BALL, BANTA, BARBER, BARD, BEALL, BARNHART, BEARD, BENNER, BIGGS, BISHOP, BLACK, BOBLETS, BOLING, BOWER, BOYD, BRASIER, BROTHERTON, BROWN, BRUBAKER, BRUMBAUGH, BUCHANAN, BUCHER, BURGESS, BUSH, BUTLER, CALES, CASE, CAMPBELL, CLEMENS, CLINE, CHAMBERS, COLE, COTTRELL, CRABILL, CRAIG, CROFT, CULTICE, DAVIS, DeCOURSEY, DETROW, DIEFENBACH, DISHER, DONALDSON, EARLY, EARLEY, EKES, ELKINS, FELIX, FILBERT, FOCHT, FOSTER, FRAME, FRANKLIN, FRITZ, FRY, GARDNER, GARLAND, GAVIN, GIFFORD, GIFT, GILLETTE, GILMORE, GORDON, GRAHAM, GRAY, GREGG, GRIMES, GREENFIELD, GRIFFIN, HAMILTON, HARBAUGH, HARLAN, HARRIS, HARSHMAN, HARPER, HATHAWAY, HENDERSON, HEWIT, HEWITT, HOFFMAN, HOERNER, HOUSE, HOWARD, HUDSON, HUNT, JAMESON, JEFFERIS, JOHNSON, JONES, KELLER, KELLEY, KIRKMAN, KISLING, KOONS, KRAMER, LANE, LAFORE, LAFOURE, LEONARD, LEWELLEN, LOSH, MacDONALD, MARSH, MARSHALL, MATCHETT, McCLERKIN, McCORMICH, McDOWELL, McGAW, McLAUGHLIN, MICHAEL, MONFORT, MOTE, MOORE, MORRIS, MORROW, MURPHY, MYERS, NATION, NEILL, NEITHERCUTT, NIXON, NUSSBAUM, O'NEAL, OSTERBERGER, OSTERBURGER, PAGE, PAINTER, PARROTT, PATRICK, PATTERSON, PERKINS, PINKERTON, POSTON, PRICE, PRILL, QUINN,

RAMSEY, RAY, REED, RENO, RENAUD, RENAULT, RESSLER, REICHARD, RICHARDS, RIESER, RITZ, ROE, ROSS, RUNYON, SANDS, SAUER, SAUERLAND, SAYR, SAYRES, SEIBERT, SEITZ, SHAFER, SHEARER, SHEPARD, SHIVELY, SIGEL, SILVERS, SIMPSON, SLAUGHTER, SLOAN, SMITH, STIDHAM, STROOP, STUBBS, SURFACE, SUTTON, SWAILS, TAYLOR, THOMAS, THOMPSON, TIBBETS, TONEY, TRACY, TRIBBETT, TULLY, UTT, UTZ, VANTZ, VENA, WAGNER, WEAVER, WETZEL, WHITE, WHITEMAN, WRIGHT, YORK, YOUNG, ZEEK

About the Author

Gary L. Morris worked from 2009 to 2014 as a professional researcher for a major player in the genealogy field. After tracing his family lineage back to 1683, he found that genealogy could be an expensive undertaking. As such, has decided to publish these helpful guides to share the valuable free information he has discovered during his career to help others trace their family lineages as inexpensively as possible. An avid genealogist himself, he hopes you will find this guide factual, thorough, helpful, and most of all, effective in helping you to find your family members.

Notes

Notes